GRIEVE TO HEAL
beginnings

GRIEVE TO HEAL
beginnings

Lydia Nash

Copyright © 2022 by Lydia Nash

All rights reserved. No part of this book may be reproduced or used in any manner without written permission of the copyright owner except for the use of quotations in a book review.

Reviewers may quote brief passages.

FIRST EDITION

ISBN, paperback: 978-1-80227-460-8
ISBN, ebook: 978-1-80227-461-5

Published by PublishingPush.com

This book is typeset in Arial Narrow

To Dr Strange for saving my life; each time you walked past our covid swabbing booth during filming of Dr Strange 2, I felt reborn.

To my late father Harry, lying in an unmarked grave in Chirinda Forest, may you continue to rest in peace. To Lusas, I met you a bitter man, healed by love; I hope you finally found peace. Written with all survivors of whatever nature and degree of loss in mind. Grief is multifaceted and can be at various levels. It can be evoked by the end of a relationship, being a victim of fraud, social isolation, bullying and harassment and the climax of it all is bereavement. To those who are still to experience the deep chasm of bereavement, I hope you find guidance. When a loved one passes away, it is not the end, but positive outcomes can be achieved.

To the not-to-be-mentioned people who were around me during this period of near insanity, thank you for your support and understanding. To those who were unaware of my torment and bereft state and who were unfortunate enough to have been the recipients of unwarranted thoughtlessness and brash behaviours portrayed unintentionally and intentionally towards you leaving you baffled and emotional bruised, I am now able to say sorry. Gracias to my comfort being, Benadryl Cool-catch-it; you kept me going. I love your acting and everything else about you.

Disclaimer

The book is based on the journey of the writer in mitigating pain after a bereavement. The writer experienced the death of a friend whilst trying to make sense of bullying and harassment in the workplace and a job loss. Based on true events but furnished with added 'spice' to make it interesting enough to hold your attention. I would like to qualify myself as a grief expert as I have experienced catastrophe after catastrophe. Catastrophe knows me by name. However, I have realised managing bereavement is individual-based and requires a far deeper understanding of interpersonal dynamics and the temerity of life itself. Some events or people descriptions may appear to fit you; this might be by accident.

Contents

Chapter 1 9

Chapter 2 15

Chapter 3 21

Chapter 4 33

Chapter 5 39

Chapter 6 45

Chapter 7 53

Chapter 8 67

Chapter 9 - Healed 91

Chapter 1

September 2019, the sky was a clear blue hue. Rays of sunlight slashed across the lawn of the garden and filtering through the open windows into the house. It was comfortably warm, and a person would sweat in this weather only after the exertion of manual labour. The garden, an oxygen factory, was about 500 square meters and was all grass, lushly green with a few patches of red mounds from squirrels and other underground animals. I love green patches a lot; they scream of life-saving oxygen and create an air of tranquillity. Occasionally, I enjoyed walking in the garden barefoot to enjoy the soft cushion of turf caressing my feet. Lusas religiously cut the grass once a month even though, inside me, I wished he would leave the grasses to enjoy their life span until they withered and dried up. This was the dream of a woman who grew up mostly in wild and forest Africa. I could hear different bird songs emanating from the large trees acting as the fence. The songs created a happy and cheerful environment, enveloping me with a facade of happiness. Surreptitiously, I gazed at Lusas, my boyfriend, and saw him grin sheepishly with a slight hint of mischief. There was a twinkle in his eyes, and I never could resist such. He had just been in the garden mowing grass, and I had helped mowing and putting away the grass debris into the brown bin. Lusas then announced that he was going to have a shower. He was walking about the bedroom with a slight limp like a cockerel in the presence of a hen on heat. With his forefinger, he pointed at me and then at the bathroom. I knew I was being summoned. Lusas was naked save for his bathrobe which was suggestively open at the front. His sweaty skin glistened like some traditional castor oil had been spread generously on his body. His skin was glistening with sweat and, as someone who was exceptionally good with his personal hygiene, no unpleasant odour was emanating from his person. The house was empty of any other soul save for us. Upon entering the bathroom, Lusas grabbed me and started kissing and caressing me. Despite being an expert in bedroom antics, Lusas's kiss always left me baffled. He would just place his mouth hard against yours with a slightly open mouth. He was borderline obsessive-compulsive disorder, and this dictated his kisses. I suppose my mouth was always screaming germs. Lusas then released me to remove his bathrobe, this was a queue for me to eliminate all forms of barrier. He was charged with an ardour matching no other man I have known. I was amazed at his energy, and, in my mind, I was refuting the age-old stereotyping of 'younger woman with older man gold-digger' label. Older men, in my mind, now appeared more energised, and, with gained experience, knew how to explore the female body making it boil and erupt like a volcano with ecstasy. With a nudge, I was brought to the present by Lusas who was getting more impatient by the minute. We both sauntered into the shower cubicle. It was like a dive into paradise, a land of dreams, our secret rendezvous where our bodies would become one with warm water, its pressure as it fell creating a rhythm heightening desire and a yearning for fulfilment. The warmth of the water was like an aphrodisiac for Lusas, transforming him into a king of passion. This was his favourite moment in all the history of his sex life, he had told me. I knelt like a servant unto his master and employed age-old techniques. This is the moment where pagan drums would be echoing sensual tempos. The dance unique to the two of us, the drums can be heard pitching higher and higher and then just a dull thud. End of the dance. He shook and groaned as if an electric shock was passing through his body. As the spasms shook his body, he held strongly onto the rails in the shower to prevent him from slipping and falling. I looked at him glowing with pride and satisfaction. For a 70-year-old man, Lusas had the sexual appetite of a beginner, an explorer, and he wanted it daily. Our sex life was very adventurous, guided by his experienced gathered over 50 years. Lusas went for it like there was no tomorrow. Unbeknown to me, he had to enjoy himself till the end. He harboured a secret. I was a thespian in a one foot in the grave saga and I did not have a script to this biopic.

As we left the bathroom, with renewed vigour and slight hint of tiredness from spent passion, I travelled back in time to September 2020. We first met at his friend's birthday party. We sat side by side by design as his wife's friend was matchmaking us. Throughout the party, we would steal glances at each other and appeared to like one another. During dinner, Lusas was the gentlemen, and he would feed me from his plate. Galant gentleman, well-travelled, knowledgeable with a lot of experiences to share. From then on and thus began our story, shared triumphs, and failures. One memorable act from my Lusas was that he offered me accommodation when I was homeless. At first, he indicated that it would be temporary until I could find my own place. With failed attempts to secure my own habitat, Lusas said I could live with him until further notice.

I am not an angel. There were dark secrets in my history that marred our union. I used gambling as a maladaptive coping strategy for pain and stress. This began when I was sexually assaulted at work in December 2018. I had intentions of quitting work and a 'boyfriend' groomed me. After the assault, I was depressed, and this gambling recruiter boyfriend invited me to the seaside. I thought he was a gallant gentleman helping a damsel in distress. Amos his name was. Amos won a lot of money during the seaside trip, and I stupidly thought I could also make a living doing such. I was taken hook, line and sinker. Luckily, I know the detriments of gambling through my work and understand that it is all chance. One in a million wins while the majority loses. Gambling to me is just a pleasant pastime which should be stopped when you are losing more than you can spare. I have always felt an emptiness and shame after losing money during gambling. There is always a rush of adrenaline as I am winning and after a climax, the game starts losing. An addict will continue to play with the intention of winning. My favourite game is the dolphin pearls. I have realised I got hooked by just seeing the dolphins lining up in threes to give a feature. It can be addictive and leads to the loss of a lifetime's savings and relationships. Gambling, I have learned through experience, creates distrust in a relationship. A partner will think this gambler might gamble my money away.

Lusas thought I was homeless and in debt due to gambling. I only went gambling once while living with Lusas.

Lusas was exceptionally good with money, and he encouraged me to pay off my debts and this I did. He was my financial hero. His belief was no debt, no credit card, and no loans. He worked as a debt collector for some 'company', and, on Tuesdays, he worked at a friend's carpet shop. On Thursday night, he attended practice with his friend in preparation for music gigs. I used to marvel at his energy and his motto was 'work and get the pound.'

Lusas enjoyed sex in the morning. When having sex, the clock above the bed would strike the hour about five times. Through it all, I would wait for the clock strikes as this would signify my release from passion land. I am not frigid; the ardour, the coordination, body movements took every ounce of my being. Anyone who looks down on an elderly man, shut up and go geriatric. It will be a pornographic movie with all the Kama Sutra styles covered.

So went the days of our lives - baths, bed, and long-playing exchange of bodily fluids. However, I have changed my mind about age in a relationship. Age is just a number; chemistry, understanding and love count.

Chapter 2

Lusas had a passion for making me jealous. He enjoyed chatting with the opposite sex. The trap was to be a possessive psycho girlfriend with insecurities. Despite feeling insecure, I was respectful of him and wished for him to be happy in his later years. I had sacrificed myself to make him happy and remove all the bitterness he held about women. Lusas did not trust women. He attributed this to the events that led to the demise of his marriage. He felt cheated and robbed of his finances. He indicated that he had been suicidal in the early days of his divorce. He had to resort to therapy from one of his psychotherapist friends. My observation of his contact with some people bordered on suicidality. He had no qualms in eating with friends and foe. My Lusas, my angel.

I am a deeply religious person, and I am very prayerful whilst Lusas believed in spirits. He did not believe in God and forbade me to pray in the house. I have healing hands and have observed that my body accepts a problem from a person and, if I do not pray and release the problem, it will stick with me, be it homelessness, joblessness, spirit of harlotry, bad omens, or sickness. I went exercising one day with a friend who was known for sexual disinhibitions. When I got home, I flashed my breasts to Lusas and his friend. A demon manifesting in me, I was doomed. At work, a very spiritual patient whom I had rapport with chased me calling me 'wh're.' I got my leg injured and was not able to attend for work.

Next day, I was on the streets. I cried night and day and tried to call Lusas, but he never answered. Heartbreak, like bereavement, can culminate in some physical pain. The pain was in my chest. I do empathise with all the people who are heartbroken in any fashion. I have seen in the news stories of men killing their spouses for cheating. This is grieving gone wrong. When walking, you can slip either backward or forward. It is just a small mishap; it does not warrant you completing the fall. Through the disillusionment that is cutting you to pieces, a moment of reality check is imperative. My reality was 'I came from my mother's womb as a single entity.' I tend to appreciate the time that God had allowed me to enjoy a relationship and when time has been called on it, I soldier on. Relationships are meant to be an institution of joy and sharing of life experiences with the ability to reconcile on your differences. Continuous Baghdad war-zone relationships are toxic, so accept defeat as a beginning. In my formulations, I always say endings and beginnings and not beginnings and endings. An optimistic approach.

There is no art to reading the mind in the construction of the face. Lusas had the intention of me going to the council and pleading homelessness when he decided to leave his house to his son. One afternoon, I found all my clothes on the ground outside the house. There was a note saying I had been evicted. Hue, a friend of mine, picked me up from Lusas's. I stayed overnight at Hue's and spent two weeks before finding shared accommodation. I was heartbroken and I felt dead. I loved Lusas with all my heart, and I felt like I had failed him dismally. In my myopic brain, I had envisioned my relationship with Lusas to be my last relationship.

At the time he left my life, permanently 'died', we were incredibly good friends. I respected him and, at times, I allowed myself to dream of us getting married after the COVID pandemic.

The pandemic hit us in March 2020. I advised Lusas to isolate as I had heard of the vulnerability of the elderly. In the early days, he was faithful in avoiding contracting the virus. I was affected drastically by the pandemic, experiencing news of mortality and morbidity daily.

Mortality defines men, born with a life span and a 'half-life.' Each day is eating away into that ration that the creator bestows on us. I was not born with an awareness of death, but a robust cry, signifying a gusto for what mother earth can avail me. The historic COVID-19 pandemic altered my life significantly. It is like living with a timer, 'tick-tock,' 'tick-tock.' Recently, I have become more aware of this looming dark cloud circling over each one of us like a vulture; an insatiable vulture grabbing and snatching away helpless prey. Living through COVID 19 and its variants from March 2020 to 2022 has demonstrated the fragility of life and how it can be snuffed out by an invisible, tiny, microscopic organism. Daily, we wait for the announcements of the statistics for deaths and the infected, checking the news and the direct gov. website for information and guidance and looking for tips to evade the invisible killer. People breathing in the same air, some are infected, and some are not. Scientists are working hard to unravel the mystery of this virus. This checking for statistics has since developed from a habit to a 'hobby' which I do not particularly enjoy. It is now like an addiction; I must know, but after finding out, a sense of dread engulfs me. The figures started low but began to rise like a creeper plant with a high growth rate strategically planted on the base of a very tall pole. As of 02/02/2022, two years later, statistics for the UK stand at 157 000 deaths with 17.4million cases. We are slowly graduating from a pandemic to an endemic.

During the biblical times, there are records of plagues and deaths, and this is recorded in Numbers 25:9 – "*And those that died in the plague were twenty and four thousand.*"

One tends to wonder about the origin of COVID; can it be explained by chronicles of the book of Chronicles which explains plagues as the hand of God? We know the virus originated from China. I am hesitant and fearful to ascribe God as the reason for this pandemic as I might be accused of blasphemy. Those things I do not understand of the deity, I desist from making conclusions and judgements. What I know is sometimes God does not lift the hand of the evil one upon his children.

Death is an inevitable visitor whose appearance is seldom welcome. A thief, stealth in its ways. 'May their soul rest in peace' - a robotic reaction from sympathisers. Where do deceased souls go? This brings a conundrum of theories, dreamy escapist 'sugar candy mountain' versions..... 'is now an angel, fly high.'... 'is in paradise where there are no fears'. Being a Christian, I subscribe to the latter.

Lydia Nash

In the Shona Language, they say *'zvairwadza vasara,'* meaning the people left behind do suffer the pain and ultimate consequences of a death. Daily, I harbour the feeling that we are that generation or population that God has forgotten. These are fleeting thoughts and are not sustained. I know there is a God in heaven working night and day to right the wrongs that human activity created. Faith and hope held firmly and guarded jealously. For some have given up and committed suicide. For me, suicide is a luxury. I have a responsibility of love and support for family and friends. I aim not to play a hand in intentionally causing grief to my loved ones.

Chapter 3

My one-year relationship with Lusas has been the best part of my life. Prior to that and outside that, hell has always awaited me, like a large vacuum hole ready to suck me in. Living a life of perpetual disarray, confusion and hatred created a loner in me. I have been moulded into an isolated inhabitable compacted island. I envision me as a rocky island like Gibraltar. The rock of Gibraltar brings joy and wonder in people's souls. I appear to bring out the worst in people. My '*Idi*' is a protected hardened rock, undefeated. My real self, the '*ego*' is an exceptionally soft loving dog. I love without reservations when true love and friendship are on the menu. One major shortfall I have is that I get disappointed to breaking point when people play Judas Iscariot, the betrayer.

I am the most misunderstood human being on earth. This part of being misunderstood I will explore in another book if, after this attempt, I can 'hazard' another book. I have become a subject of hate and ridicule. People formulate theories about me and sometimes assess them by subjecting me to disrespectful acts. Some people thought I was a vampire and wanted to do away with me. There appears to be another theory that I cannot eat in public. I have been labelled a racist, witch, wh.. re, drug dealer. My current stance is, if you have a label, stick it on. People's perceptions of me cannot be altered by force; if there is no confrontation, I owe nobody any explanation. I aim to please God and not to harm people. I have adopted a habit of forgiveness. Grudges eat away your core leaving you bitter with accompanying physical and psychological illnesses borne of stress.

I have had people I related to during the pandemic. Pena, a 43-year-old coloured woman from the 'Teapot Nation', Zimbabwe, was my prayer partner at the start of the pandemic. She also played a significant part when I was defrauded. However, without much elaboration, I would like to say some wise people are their own friends. For it is the one who has the privilege to be in your life that can destroy your life. There are hyenas in sheep's skin, and the irony of it is that if a person close to you spreads lies about you, people believe them as your friend is deemed a primary witness. This is in addition to neighbours; they are deemed primary witnesses. A rumour was spread that

I was killing people as I was crying. For neighbours who are very observant, I started crying when many people were dying, asking God to help us. I went through a transformation and God showed me some verses to read, from the books of Leviticus and Revelations. I did not understand at first. However, I started noticing a trend. If I did not pray, the statistics would be higher. I started cancelling shifts to pray. For my prayer, I used two white prayer cloths. These cloths were highly anointed as they have the anointing I received when God gave me the powers. In the Bible, the prophet was told to make an image of the regions and make some barricades to protect the regions. The prophet was advised to lie on alternating sides until God deemed it time for him to get up. He was advised to have his food there and just lie down praying. I also followed the same advice with my laptop and barricaded with staff, I was praying fervently in spirit, and at times, the spirit appeared so angry and asking God what kind of a father he was. I was scared and would just cower and keep quiet. I was crying loudly at times, and I was assaulting my neighbours' ears daily.

God, on several occasions, instructed me to make figurines of a virus. I would use bread and then I would pray that the virus be weak and throw it in the toilet. In my prayers, the spirit would guide me to just spread healing to the four corners of the world, so I did this on daily basis. I convulse at times, even in public places. This is when I become prayerful; I am not withdrawing from any illegal substances.

Back to my prayer cloths. I now have one. One was stolen on the 13th of December between my home and a cruise at Southampton Port. The same tactic was used to steal my work badge and a lanyard which I was using to hold my identification badges.

Through my work as a swabber, I have experienced a lot of people attempting to be healed hence I was touched periodically despite social distancing guidance. Some had ideations that I could grow their bum. Oh dear; you wonder where this was coming from. The loss of my cloth appeared to have weakened me. Them collecting my clothing was like them taking my underwear. I vowed celibacy to God.

Some reactants in either the soap or the tissues used in one cruise ship I worked on made my private parts itch horribly. I scratched but did not succumb to fornication. Men were assigned to clean my cabin daily despite me being a crew member and that my room was only to be cleaned once a week.

I had become very observant to anomalies and at times, I would question the validity of my assumptions and my sanity. I felt like they wanted to transfer the superpowers to someone else as I was deemed unworthy.

Whilst I was in cruise ship two, coronavirus deaths were increasing, but I could not pray the way I normally pray. However, upon coming back I prayed. Zimbabwe was easier for me to have my prayers answered. In the UK, Meghan Markle was ostracised and deemed unworthy. Then Caroline Flack committed suicide and the are two of the people in our care that we are mistreating. Even if it was the hand of Caroline Flack that finally did the job, society killed her. People judging people by who they date. Is there anything wrong in dating a younger man?

Racism is rife in the United Kingdom. People are trained from a tender age. It also appears as if black people are perpetuating racism unknowingly. A black colleague falsely reporting a black colleague; manna from heaven from the bosses. There would not be any sympathy. Companies with black managers are used to discrimination against their peers. Racism can be subtle, especially if there is another black leader in the 'pack.'

We are grieving......................

Back to the pandemic, I also joined a prayer group which belonged to Lucy's church. The prayer sessions were done every three hours. During these sessions, people known to be unwell, and the world at large was prayed for. People were very sombre but prayed fervently, trying to will God to save loved ones and to make the world safe. During challenging times, people are known to make covenants with God. I vowed and made a covenant to desist from sex until the pandemic stops.

God is known to be a covenant fulfiller. Leviticus 26:42 "***Then I will remember my covenant with Jacob and my covenant with Isaac, and my covenant with Abraham will I remember, and I will remember the land.***"

Ezekiel 16:60 "***Nevertheless I will remember my covenant with thee with thee in the days of thy youth and I will establish unto thee an everlasting covenant***".

I am single at 47. This is due to my spirituality and tendency to sit on a higher than optimal moral high ground. My name is Lydia Nash, and I am from the 'teapot' nation. I have experienced grief at various multifaceted levels. Being single is like a death, buried within the corners of my abode with no other soul to connect to. I have found it incredibly challenging to find a serious boyfriend post-divorce. I was married to my ex-husband for 20 years and irreconcilable differences meted the union its demise. A couple of non-serious sporadic liaisons followed. Believe you me, the non-seriousness was not being emitted from my part. It appeared as if I was walking about with a 'marry me' rudder that pushed men away. Having travelled overseas, I failed to wash off my adult-acquired very conservative outlooks on life. Especially important to me is the marriage institution and I used to strongly believe a woman is whole with a husband. This conservative culture-borne ideation can be explored to various conclusions by different people but that is not the gist of the story and hence I will endeavour to pursue my theme.

Lusas was a 70-year-old white male who originally hailed from Austria at a tender age. We met through my workmate Lucy. Lucy told me that Lusas was 60 years old and had been single for five years after a very nasty divorce from his ex. Upon meeting Lusas, we connected immensely. Lusas, from my loved-up eye, had a striking resemblance to Robert DeNiro; to be more precise, a shorter Robert DeNiro who was so good at playing bass guitar that his bass made me fall irrevocably in love with him. The first day I attended his show, I was bedazzled and was taken hook, line and sinker. His other sexy trait was his strength, physically and emotionally. Lusas continued to play music until he moved on to the next world. He used very heavy equipment which he carried single-handedly. He fell once while transferring his equipment but did not flinch. In a martyr-like fashion, he continued, assuring me he was fine and advising me not to carry heavy loads. He was a hero, a knight in shining armour. However, at times, I would feel a sense of sadness, pity and empathy when looking at him; he was sacrificial. Despite being very masculine when naked, when clothed, he appeared dainty with a slight hint of femininity. At 70, Lusas had maintained his body shape to admirable standards. My heart would skip a beat when looking at him. He had a bit of a roving eye, but I took it with reservations; questioning his activities appeared to be like asking a baby why they are wriggling their toes - being sociable was second nature.

Apart from his alluring physique, Lusas took me in when I was stranded. I joined Maleca hospital as a nurse in 2018, and, for six months, I was on emergency tax. After paying rent, I ended up with no food. I would buy a packet of lemon creams for dinner. I was attracted to Maleca hospital by a gross annual income of 43000 pounds. Take home was eight hundred pounds and my rent was 850 pounds for a one-bedroom flat. Subsequently, I became thin and emaciated and looked like a very slender model. This was one trait Lusas admired in a woman, his main deal-builder. Due to some technical errors with the renting company, there was confusion with my flat occupation date. Despite explaining that I got paid on the first, they declined to adjust the dates leading to them evicting me. Lusas granted me permission to reside at his 3-bed semi-detached property until I had stabilised. Of all the people in the United Kingdom, Lusas was the only person who gave me a place to stay. Others would want to date me and did not want to know my troubles.

Lusas was very jocular and found humour in the silliest of things. As I am writing, I can envision him vividly standing in front of the mirror mimicking my antics when checking out my bum. Lusas was exceptionally soft spoken, easy to talk to and never shouted at me. He was very attentive on and off the bed. He had this insatiable love for people and had the ability to keep friendships.

When I started living with Lusas, he would take me to work daily until I bought my own car. When I could not cook, he would cook; he was an exceptionally good cook. His speciality was French fries and pork belly. He liked to also make some delicacies his Austrian mum used to make for him. For a grown-up man, he had very fond memories of his mum which was very admirable. He wore a ring in memory of his mum. Lusas helped me to save my money and pay off some debt, though of course at some point, I felt like I was working to pay off a debt. Lusas lent me 6500 pounds which I was to use to pay off debts and help me find my feet. This debt has since been paid off. He declined the offer of me paying for bills but agreed that I would buy groceries and clothes for us. Like me, he took pride in clean surroundings, and he enjoyed watching me do some house chores. He enjoyed washing cars and I also assisted him when he was doing so. He was my role model, my knight in shining armour. He walked stealthy and never made some noise despite being quick-paced. At times, I would be amazed at how he moved from my side to somewhere else. Lusas was noticeably clear that he was too old to marry but I considered him to be my husband and respected him as such, as, in the Shona culture, once you live with a man they say *'watizira.'* This was a reality for me but rubbish for him. This became a joke in our lives. We were happy until some love rival worked voodoo on me. I also suspect that Lucy's other friend, Rebecca, lied about me. Rebecca and I were involved in each other's lives for a year. I avoid the word friends, but I can use the word pseudo friends. Rebecca introduced me to online dating and was also encouraging me to join the ones for casual dating for money. That was when I took my life back and removed myself from Rebecca's life. People think I was wh..re. I have never had two boyfriends at one time. Of course, I have dated people which is normal but if they do not marry me and prefer their other sweethearts, whose fault would it be? To cut a long story short, I loved Lusas and wondered whether he would have looked my way had I met him ten years earlier; something to consider.

One thing that always troubled me was his grandchildren who were squatting in some camp, and I used to ask whether the man he called son was his real son. Me being prudish, I expected them to be living together and the son to inherit the house. He was talking about the son inheriting his mother's house. Through talking, he adopted my point of view. However, I envisaged trouble if the two families lived together. Eventually, father and son had a discussion, and I was evicted by the uncle. This was maybe because I had told him that because I was earning enough, I could rent. I just did not expect it to be sudden.

I grieved in 2019 when I broke up with Lusas. I had a sore leg and did not have any place to go.

Lydia Nash

Chapter 4

Scammed: The sensation of death

It never rains but it pours, a cliché but so apt for my poor soul. During this pandemic, I was defrauded of all my life savings. No single person believed my story and the loss was like a death itself.

On September 8, 2020, I received an email inviting me to activate my trading account with T1 markets. The website is very plausible with a blue background. I mention blue because it is my favourite colour. My colleagues at work had been talking about trading and I was eager to experience this game-changer money-making scheme. On this date, I did not open an account.

How I lost my money appears to be a case of stupidity on my part. Believe you me, it is not the case. In September, I was working in Maleca ward as a nurse. On one night, I had a misunderstanding with one male colleague who was very loud-mouthed. I was so stressed, I felt hated and discriminated against. I felt like I had had enough of nursing. So, it was like a Godsend opportunity when Shakar V from T1 markets offered to trade in oil. I was lying in bed stressed when I received his call. Well, when a sheep is to be slaughtered, it does not know but follows the lead humbly and trustingly. I was that sheep. A person hungry and desperate for a way out of poverty and the damningly stressful job. Manna from heaven, I thought, never fell so hard and abundantly. My manna was here at last. My sugar candy mountain. My breakthrough. Unbeknown to me, there have been many cases of people being defrauded of money. The pandemic made many people jobless and affected their finances. Some people, knowing how people were stressed and very unsure of the future, realised there was an opportunity to fill their pockets with ill-gotten gains. I had been earning an incredibly good salary from my full-time job at Maleca and had also gotten a handsome tax rebate from the past four years. I had tried to put my money with NS and I premium bonds, but this did not happen. My money floated for three days and was returned to my bank account. I had opened some trading accounts with other companies, and I was still testing waters.

Back to my broker, Shakar V; he called me on September 8, 2020, and asked me to activate my account. To do that, I had to deposit 250 pounds. I did so. My intention was to allow the 250 pounds to grow through trades. On the sixteenth of September, Shakar V called me and told me about the forecast for oil post-Covid. He had my back. He, like a sleek snake, slithered into my brain and filled it with hope. This was my undoing, the words that lured me like rat into a nut-filled trap.

The words 'let us do this and you will thank me later' still ring like a death knell.

That life-changing moment that creeps up on you, seemingly dripping with sweet cream, but underneath, full of cyanide.

Shakar V persuaded me to deposit all my life savings of 20 000 ponds. He spent two hours working his charm on me. In the end, I was sold.

He then advised me to trade in oil, Nasdaq, and others. He then advised me to hedge my trade. This was buying and selling the same stock in substantial amounts. At some point, he called me and indicated that I would get more rewards if I upgraded my account. To upgrade, I had to complete some forms. One was acknowledging that I had done ten trades and he advised me to add more trading positions which I did. Another form was to the effect that I had about five hundred thousand to invest which I did not have. I told him this was a lie and he said it did not matter.

He made me redo the training needs form and he advised me to put down some erroneous information indicating that I was a very experienced trader. I was telling him that it was not fine putting in erroneous information, but he reassured me that all was well. He indicated that hedging does not affect equity. As a green trader, I was sold. What happened after is a nightmare, an apocalyptic catastrophe happening during the Covid-19 apocalypse. I watched, dazed and stricken, as my money was being churned away and the equity going lower and lower. I called Shakar and he said I should add more money. I said I had no money and he said put in an overdraft, so I organised a 4 000-pound overdraft. He then said to save my money I had get a loan and put it in. I tried to get a loan and could not get it. I asked him why he gave me bad advice, but he told me, "I never told you anything. You made the decision yourself". I did not sleep for two days watching the money being swallowed. At some point, the trades just closed, and all my money was gone.

What followed were frantic attempts to get hold of Shakar but he never answered my calls. He had disappeared. I called his manager and I never got help. I called the bank telling them I was being conned and not to release some money and they did not listen. On one day, I went to the bank and was overwhelmed with the pain of many losses. I just broke down and started wailing. I threw myself on the ground as the pain was crumpling my body. No one was listening. Up to now, I have only recovered 7 000 pounds. In January 2022, I visited that site and there was ten thousand in the account. I could not believe my eyes. To check whether it was real money, I traded a little, making money. When I tried to withdraw it, I could not. The account was changed to a demo account a few days later.

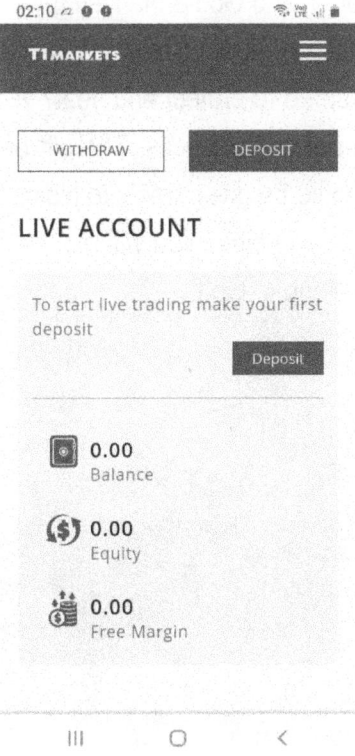

From 24 000 to zero. The detriments of get-rich-quick deals. I was the walking dead after this. Prayer helped me to be able to move from the limbo of grief. I lost my job and had to live on benefits.

In January 2021, I started another job Covid-testing and, in my soul, I was praying for the company that hired me. I became even more prayerful, and God enhanced my powers of healing. I would seem like an angel of mercy. Do you know what the blood of Jesus can do to protect and heal? Well, Jesus healed me from the pain of many losses. The gift of healing is a gift from God and should be given freely to his children. It is only a happy person who can bless you with something when happy. Silver and gold belong to God.

Chapter 5

While this was happening, the Covid-19 pandemic continued. At some point, the spirit of God opened my eyes. The virus was no longer the one killing people; it was adverse reactions from vaccines. Fortunately, I got an invite to attend for a Covid jab at a hospital that was doing trials for the Pfizer vaccine. The night before the appointment, I prayed fervently asking God to make the vaccines safer with lesser life-threatening side effects. I woke up early on the day of the appointment. I took the necessary documentation and one of my prayer cloths. As I was driving towards Carshalton, I was listening to gospel music on my car radio and bursting into spirit-filled prayer.

I arrived well before the appointment time. I went round and round in circles in the neighbouring residential areas looking for suitable parking. Round in circles is an understatement. The roads were packed with cars parked on any suitable space. A spot appeared conveniently in proximity to the hospital. I stayed in my car praying. As my time was nearing, I left the car with my prayer cloth draped on my shoulders. I said, "God, I am here, help".

I went in and got my jab and while waiting in the post-jab observation area, I was praying silently. I was asking God to make the jabs safe for people. If it was not to be case, well, I was ready for it to kill me as well. Thirty minutes later, no reactions except the pain on the injection site, and all the other people who were being observed were safe. I left the hospital still praying.

To some people, I might appear formidable and, as such, unapproachable. Inside, I hunger to be understood and I am fragile. I imagine myself as a lion in an inferno-destroyed vlei' The fire-devastated vlei is bare, devoid of sources of nourishment and hence in a state of starvation. I envisage the human soul as requiring the nourishment of being treated like a human being.

If I were to take a step back, imagine myself as a plant, I would be a withered and shrivelled plant. A neglected rose living a life of misery and ultimate exclusivity. I remember a time when I had friends, but it is like a hazy, distant memory. I feel like I have accidentally taken a trip onto another planet. In this planet, I have not been accepted, but been viewed as an alien. The lonely souls may drown in the underworld of illicit solicitations and habits to curb a hunger for some form of control and belonging. It is in this vulnerable state that some people embrace fake extended hands of friendship and cling to them despite the risk of exploitation and possible emotional and physical harm.

This feeling of being marginalised, loss and pain, whether real or a created illusion borne from a need to survive and get by, can create an urgent desire to unleash the dragon onto a clean white slate. Hence began the journey of most renowned writers, a position as which I had been yearning for and eager to conquer from a tender age. Grief transformed me into an active volcano, read to unleash lava. Death had triggered the active button, transforming me into a force ready to launch a missile of words hoping it would make sense and help others as they amass word after word of my untrained armature journey. It is weird that for me, the death of my friend marred my perception of past/present amalgamating all the deaths I had experienced into my life making the pain more so unbearable and some would not understand. During my mourning period, a once in a lifetime opportunity to work on a cruise ship rendered me emotionally charged and ready to unleash, and I felt more considered. I felt at one with the vast open and merciless volumes of innocent but treacherous waters. The need for release churned in my core like I had never felt before; words tumbled out of my mind and translated into the tip-top of my laptop. I felt a joy through my pain and a sense of the beginning of realisation of a lifetime dream that had begun as child when I was made responsible of the grade 6 library at the age of ten. Writing can be a means or an end to productive grieving.

The complexity of grieving is more of a mystery and a sacred conversation which most dare not tread upon. Ironically, the only way to experience grief is through living through it. Families with means are now known to rear pets with short life spans and this becomes the opportunity for their offspring to experience and cope with death. The dilemma is, whether attachment to a pet can be comparable to that of a close family member and their deaths as well? There are a lot of cultural and ethical issues to explore but the main and most important standpoint is the personal nature of attachment and grief.

I am a middle-aged woman of black ethnic minority descent, hailing from a large family with the inevitable close extended parts being part of my everyday social life. Upon migration to the United Kingdom, I lost all my social connections when I left my husband due to the repeated and unbearable barrage of emotional and occasionally physical abuse. Years of silence while receiving unwarranted torment from my husband had rendered the very intrinsic me timid, shy and with extremely low levels of self-esteem. Aesthetically, I am a very pretty woman who could pass for a model despite my being vertically height-challenged - I was 5'2". My main attraction is my posterior; my bum extended from a slightly bent back giving a Kim Kardashian figure-of -eight shape which many men found very sexy. In my shame, I always covered my bum and walked with my head down most times and, in any social interactions, I would be noticeably quiet, and it would be a miracle if I were to reply with even one single syllable. My eventual and lifesaving disengagement from this detrimental matrimonial situation adversely impacted on my social life as I had geographically distanced myself from family friends. The single female friend who had stayed in contact with me, appeared to have had an advantage through the partnership; I was assisting her with her schoolwork. This not so symbiotic relationship expired when I separated with my ex-husband. Surprisingly, the reason might have stemmed from the fact that within most conservative African societies, single ladies are perceived as threats to the matrimonial bliss of those tenacious or lucky enough to be able to create and maintain a still-surviving institution of marriage. These circumstances, therefore, are a red flag to social isolation and increased vulnerability during crises. As a typical Miss 'Haversham' minus the wedding gown, I sojourned alone in a rented flat where the rules stated I could not keep any pet. Within the walls of my humble abode, I would always be in solitude with an occasional visit from ex-boyfriend turned friend, Lusas. I was emotionally attached to Lusas as we were compatible in most ways. Gentle and always harbouring a twinkle in his eye, I had never witnessed an angry Lusas. Within the three-year span in which I had been fortunate enough to be in some form of association with him, Lusas had never raised his voice to communicate any displeasure. Humour was his forte in communicating displeasure and correction. When tragedy struck, I received the hardest shock of my life and felt more lonely, dejected, and desolate. The island had become a desert slowly morphing into a deep crater threatening to swallow and bury me.

Chapter 6

'You are but a jealousy God, for real' I wailed, loudly splashing warm water on my face. I could be heard sobbing and taking in agonised breaths as I poured out my heart to my God whom I thought would have saved the only man in the whole worldwide who would move mountains and hell fire for me. I was trying hard to breathe and the sounds coming out of me were like a chicken cackling as it was under slaughter. My eyes were a reddish hue, red and teary, giving an enraged look. My short afro hair was unkempt and as it was getting wet, was still standing out like I had been through some electric shock. I was sitting naked in my bathtub with foamy water covering the lower half of my body. As tears flowed profusely from my eyes, I continued to flap my hands wildly, hitting my face with showers of much-needed cleansing water. I felt as one with the water since, at that moment, my tears were like an angry river branching off a flooded dam during a cyclone; Unstoppable. Despite this attempt to self-sanitise, nothing could wash off the deep sense of loss and betrayal. The pain felt like a blunt sword being forced through my chest. I could not equate this pain that I was experiencing with any other experienced physical pain. The pain felt during childbirth would be more welcome as this pain would give birth to a joy and the pain of bereavement is a pain of saying goodbye, of senseless loss. What could be seen below the neck was the upper half of my large sagging breasts and these could be seen flapping up and down like uncontrollable yoyos. My pain had been ongoing for three days and I could not visualise how I would cope and be able to swim to the shore from this turbulent tumult of emotions that was consuming me to the bone. During my lifetime, I had experienced deaths in the family. My father died when I was four years old, and I did not undergo the process of bereavement as I had no idea what was going on. Then, as an adult, I had no recollection of how I processed the announcement by my mother; "Your father is dead. He has been shot and killed by the liberation struggle soldiers popularly known as '*vanamukoma*'." I vividly remembered the words, but my long-term memory evaded revisiting the emotions I felt when my own father passed on. Over the course of my life, I would cry whenever I had problems that would have been solved easily or been avoided if I had a flat. I would shed bitter tears. When Lusas passed on, my world crumbled harshly, and it felt like I had lost my father all over again. If someone could have seen me, my face was marred by a known and maintained pain which has been eating me to my core since 1979 when my father died. No one deserves to experience a life with a gap that is wide open and could have been occupied by someone to call dad, and more so, a mum. Death is inevitable and the natural course of life, but it leaves wounds and altered lives. The untimely and senseless ending of my father's life had deprived me and my siblings of quite a lot. Having to live on a measly pension shared between my father's two wives, life has not been a bed of roses and champagne, but bitter ginger and tear-inducing badly cut onion. On the demise of my father, my father's siblings collected all my father's cattle and other property of value. Before the laws had been reviewed to favour widows and orphans, it had been viewed as culturally correct for the family of the deceased to seize properties without a thought on how the deceased's immediate family would continue to fend for themselves. Involuntarily and frequently, my brain would wander along the treacherous path of wondering how life would have been had my father outlived the liberation war. The adage had it thus; 'do not cry over spilt milk.' This is not apt when what had been lost altered the course of my family's life.

I do know the circumstances of my father's death. I stand to be corrected.

1979 in the Teapot nation. We lived in Chirinda Forest as my father was the forest ranger. This was a high-paying job and Father trained for it in Chimanimani where he met my mother. Having been raised by a father who was both farmer and businessman, my father's business acumen was flawless. Harry was a short handsome man, a very charismatic man and hence a crowd and women-puller. Our house was within a gap in the forest. There was a tarred road nearby and, as kids, we used to play in the grass by the roads. It was during the Smith regime and often we would meet white soldiers. I remember vividly they used to tease my brother who had a big head for 3 years old. The soldiers would call us and give us sweets. My mum used to say the sweets were bad, but sweets were more powerful than our mother's warning. My father was an innocent man caught in the middle of a war, torn apart with no option but to do what he did which I never got to know. From the eyes of a 4-year-old, one day remain vivid in my mind. My mother was crying, and my father did not come home. When I asked her, she said, "*baba vatorwa nechikwira mahara*". *Your father has been taken by a free-for-all car.* This was the nickname given to the van-like brownish-grey vehicles white soldiers used to abduct people for interrogation. My father came back from Chibonore with bandages on his head and arms. Chibonore was an interrogation camp close to Chirinda; it was more like the Nazi concentration camps and people were tortured for information. I remember my mother told me that they used electricity to burn

Grieve to Heal

information out of people. I am not sure if this was the truth but I heard the interrogation tactics were assertive and very physical.

A few weeks after my father came back from Chibonore, my childhood was irrevocable snatched from me. It was a very dark night in 1979 in war-torn Teapot nation. We had gone to sleep early only to be woken up by some commotion outside. From where I was sleeping, I could see some light from a bonfire and many shadows of people. Most were seated and a few men, whom I got to understand were the freedom fighters, were standing holding their 'orphan and widow-maker' AK47s. *'Pasi nemutengesi'* - these were chants I still remember. People were forced to sing liberation war songs. From where I was when I peeped out, I could not see my father or mum. I did not know how much pain he suffered before they finally shot him. The shotgun sounds, I remember vividly, shook me. Having been born during the war, this was a familiar sound, however, this was close; too close.

'Tiri kuuya tichizopisa mutengesi mangwana, uyai nemunyu'
We are coming back to burn the seller tomorrow, bring salt.

Jealousy and envy have been instrumental in the demise of many in Zimbabwe with people, including friends, family or strangers, reporting each other to either side of the struggle for independence in the Teapot nation. I could hear this as if it were happening at that very moment. At five, I did not understand what was happening. Lying in bed, I had listened to the noises leading to my father's death in a detached manner. I thought it had nothing to do with me. My dreams were shattered when my mum and my father's second wife barged into the children's bedroom announcing 'your father is dead.'

I am one for forgiveness and dwelling on my father's death brings bitterness. I know I am not the only person orphaned by war activities and lawlessness. In 2021, I am in the United Kingdom and have watched my fellow Teapot nationers being deported and being discriminated against. These are the orphans you created, dear England. We are still grieving ....

My present-day reality was becoming a faded silhouette, the present and the past appearing to be merging. This was threatening to topple my brain onto the edge of insanity. Suddenly, a noise penetrated my brain jolting me into the present. The noise was welcome, drawing me from the agony and memory of a life deprived and punished through circumstances beyond my control. Throughout my adult life, my mantra had been 'Crying was a sign of weakness.' Crying was a luxury as I used to wrongly think pain was a figment only existing in the mind. Pain was an indulgence of a brain which accepts favours and empathy from a kind audience. All through my life, there has not been an empathetic audience. Crying has been senseless as there has not been any respite from a constant state of living in a precarious position of hand to mouth and having to always wonder where food for tomorrow will be from. There have been times when the family has been so destitute that we were homeless, living in one single hut as a family. Understandably, crying has not been an available option; one has to get up and grind. Cry and they laugh. With death, the reality of pain landed with a loud bang. Pain is not a figment of the medulla. It is the large elephant in the room in relationship breakups, social isolation, bullying and harassment episodes, illnesses and most horrifyingly raw, bereavement.

Back to my reality, a splash of water hit my cheek. The force of it felt like it was almost slicing my cheek.

September the 11th 2021; it had been three days of mourning by me. As if in solitary confinement, I felt like a prisoner of my own making. With each passing minute, a feeling of foreboding was playing drums as if hypnotising and drawing me into a darker cave of helplessness and depression. How I would cross over from this debilitated state to be able to recover and live without Lusas needed me to dig deeper. This had to be deeper into my resilience bag. I knew I had to borrow some coping strategies I had learnt in practice as a mental health nurse. 'Physicians heal yourself.' The coping strategies I had been devising or had read about and used to assist my patients during bereavement were still ingrained in my mind. I had used the last ounce of strength I had to clutch onto and maintain sanity.

To the untrained eye, I was a weakling who would shy away from the slightest test of strength. However, embedded in me was a wonder woman, warrior to the core; my sentiments bordered on 'I have nine lives like a cat.' I had an unquenchable thirst for fighting agitated waves and swimming to the shore despite being relentlessly squeezed and pounded by the harsh force of avenging sea gods. I knew I must lose myself to survive the harrowing pain which was clutching at my core and daring me to fall.

Chapter 7

I was aware that there are some negative and positive outcomes following bereavement. I had to mourn to heal and not complete the momentum daring me to fall. I was ready to embrace anything like a barren damsel yearning to conceive and to hold an offspring that they could call their own. The positive outcomes may include a better understanding, enhanced resilience, and personal growth. Deep inside me, I was beginning to feel an appreciation of a life once taken for granted. Every opportunity, sanctioned by the one who grants us permission to wake up from near-death slumbers taken every night, should be valued. Any opportunity to love and be loved should be hungrily savoured and ferociously fought. The hourglass of our life steadily ebbs out sand and can also be accidentally spilt unexpectedly leaving players aghast, filled to the brim with regret. As I sat there like a dazed scorned woman, in the cult movie 'Coven of Sisters', I vividly brought to my mind the many times I had been too tired to go out with Lusas. I sighed heavily, and, as if on cue, a fresh river of salty liquid glided down my dark cheeks.

'Cry, beloved queen of hearts.' I had been too absorbed in morality and spirituality to embrace what was being offered. Well, I was an 'all or nothing' woman and, at times, I bordered on feeling cold on my moral high ground. This ambivalence and moral and value dilemmas might be the sole reasons I had not been able to make a clear-cut ending to my relationship with Lusas.

In my healing process, I started by assessing my situation. What it is in me and outside of me that can help me? I had intrinsic and extrinsic factors that affected my grieving process and outcome. For starters, emotional intelligence. I tend to think I have acquired a level of emotional intelligence; the ability to identify my 'demons' and know how to collaborate with them to a positive outcome. I subscribe to stress and the vulnerability model when dealing with a crisis. Over the years, I have developed a thick skin. I have experienced a lot of 'bad' and it needs more than 'bad' to topple me.

When Lusas passed on, there were pre-existing stressors in my life - the pandemic, my late father's death, and the loss of my money. I concluded that these things that happened in the past tended to make me catastrophise my situation. This was a disadvantage to my healing as I have the perception that all was being piled on me. The planets and comets above were falling and crashing onto me. This was an 'it never rains but its pours' predicament.

I assessed my social support systems. I concluded that I had no one. Lusas was the person who was close to me and visited when he could. I knew I had to envision a life without him and knew that after mourning, I must live a life minus the joy and helpfulness Lusas brought at times.

There are a lot of activities that people can engage in, intended and unintended, while mitigating their loss. Expert guidance might be vital, that is why people resort to bereavement counselling and, through intentional activities, people are assisted to engage in meaningful activities that can facilitate positive outcomes.

During bereavement, people feel emotions that they never knew existed. Most men tend to suppress the feelings and resort to contemplative silence. Men are more prone to maladaptive coping strategies when the deceased is a close relative like an offspring, parent, sibling, or spouse. These are explored elsewhere in this narrative.

In the same vein, women can be very vulnerable as they are prone to helplessness and can enter counterproductive relationships with others. I remembered when I received the news that my elder sister had passed on. I was living with a male housemate who, upon hearing me wailing after receiving the news, attended and comforted me. I was so distraught that I bought two tickets to Africa and also hired a car for the housemate to drive. The housemate did not fork out a single cent but manoeuvred himself to boyfriend status and eventual conned me out of my savings and then cheating openly so he could be dumped when I was penniless.

The death of my sister from cancer numbed me to the core. I remember being in the plane to Africa crying now and again. My sister was buried in the rural areas at my in-law's homestead. On seeing my brother-in-law, I wailed uncontrollably and felt as if the ground was being lifted off my feet when I went to the grave. Then, as if one catastrophe was not enough, the car got stuck in the mud while they were leaving the homestead. It was finally released after many men from the neighbourhood attended. They required money and I forked out. Whilst bereaved, the capacity to make the right choices can be impaired. I should not have hired the expensive car or brought the conman. Anyway, we learn that even when distressed, we should think twice, consult and act.

I reached out to a portable mirror in the bathroom. To reach this, I had to get up, as I was so grief-stricken that even the motion of standing up appeared to be a mammoth task sapping away any remaining energy reserve. I held onto the rail on the right side of the bathtub and nearly slipped but the worn-out bathmat still had some life in it and prevented my involuntary feet from moving which threatened to topple me from my vertical position. Upon getting me upright, I resumed the sitting position in the bathtub.

On this day, I cursed the inventor of mirrors. What I was staring at I could not recognise, and this startled me to the core. Tears were flowing down my puffed cheeks like an unstoppable river. I stared in wonder as I suddenly had a vision of how tears magically appear in reaction to unbearable pain. They are like an outlet of the excess emotional damage due to unfavourable experiences. It was like an outlet of all the bad and pain despite them being with no colour. They got colour as they mixed with accompanying mucus which always chose to flow when people are distressed and crying. I have not had the opportunity to research the effect of distress and pain on the mucus glands and as I looked at myself, that seemed to be of significance. God created the human body with its organs and systems and how it works was up to him; definitely when these organs should stop working and what was called a person just becomes a 'body', 'the body' a lifeless heap of organs. It was easy for the one in charge up there but not so easy for whoever is left behind.

As I continued to stare at my grief-ravaged face, my crying picked up a new tempo. A high-pitched guttural wail which appeared to be coming from a constricted throat and hence the larynx was comprised. It was an emotional agonised cry. When crying emotionally, people are at their most vulnerable and weak, but this can be a source of strength. My face looked like a picture advertising an apocalyptic horror movie. I looked ugly, and I threw away the mirror and my body involuntarily keeled over, and I clutched my belly and continued to moan. People cry despite the aesthetic effects; people can be at their ugliest as some wail and their faces contort or mouths widen or change shape accordingly. There are few people who can be called pretty whilst emotionally crying and sobbing and mourning at the same time. There are some people who just feel the emotions inside and tears just flow down their cheeks and there is no movement of face and body. These can be in some catatonic state, tragical traumatised by their loss.

There is still a need for research as to the origin or function of emotional tears. Theories range from the simple, such as response to inflicted unbearable pain. This is the focus of my attention in this narrative, an exploration of managing pain especially during a bereavement. Similarities can also be drawn to the pain you experience during a relationship break-up.

It is imperative to delve into the negative outcomes of bereavement. Bereavement is emotionally taxing and some people, despite seeking all forms of support, may be clinical depressed. For those with pre-existing mental health problems, relapse is inevitable. I had observed a fellow African lady who had lost her dear father wailing and crying on Facebook and exhibiting some behaviours indicating mental health unwellness. This lady appeared to be hallucinating and presenting herself on social media clad in traditional clothes chanting and ululating. Times like these are so much more difficult for people in the diaspora as there might be no immediate family to notice early signs of unwellness, where early intervention is particularly important in preventing deterioration in the mental state.

For married couples, bereavement may lead to neglect of each other's intimacy needs leading to breakdown of relationships. During a period of homelessness, I had rented a room from a married man who was living alone as the wife had deteriorated in her mental state and the husband had shipped the wife back to their home country; according to the husband, the wife was' useless.' Upon enquiry as to what was meant by being useless, the man would say, "I was always sleeping, could not cook, wash properly and even prepare for the needs of remaining offspring necessitating me to be looked after by my family". What the man was unwilling to explore was the possibility that his wife had been so affected by the death of her child that she was depressed and needed the input of the mental health services.

During bereavement, people also resort to seeking thrills. One example vivid in my mind was the misuse of drugs by my property owner. Children are particularly important to their father and more so sons as they are the heirs. The blow of having their apple taken away drives away any capability of the brain to explore the predicament and reach a painless destination. It is mostly gloom and drugs, and casual sex may become a refuge.

Pain is felt by an individual and can be shared when communicated. Crying is this nonverbal communication in order to elicit altruistic helping behaviours from others. Crying can be viewed as a natural God-given self-help tool or do it yourself therapy. It is a cheaper option to a psychotherapist and hospital admission. To some, it is the first go-to form of therapy. You might need a shoulder to cry on, but at times, such as when there is a coronavirus pandemic, the accompanying advice and necessary social distancing, that is not available. Wail and work it out if you feel like it, but the dilemma is - can we be sensitive to the amount of disturbance we cause to the neighbour? In African countries, wailing alerts the neighbours of a death and they flock. As word spreads, friends and relatives come wailing and even those who do not feel any loss wail. There is a joke that people decide who goes in the front when approaching the homestead of the mourning family, the most dramatic wailer being strategically positioned at the front. The procession of women will come wearing head scarfs and *zambias* over their day dresses. This is culturally a show of respect. Each woman will be carrying a 'mutani' or basin with either mealie meal, cabbage or whatever can be used for food at the funeral. It is the community sharing the pain.

Men are men and do not wail at funerals; instead, they are seen mostly with sombre faces and hiding their pain. They appear to not have a code of dress and they gather around a fireplace and share some beers, celebrating a life together and sharing the pain with the bereaved family.

Sometimes, no comforting thoughts or persons can appease this urgent need to cry and self-cleanse/heal. Crying is natural and helps people to process their pain, let go and allow the pain to wash over them. It is a moment of weakness that every human being succumbs to when any emotion regulation techniques in the book cannot help. Crying is safer than most coping strategies that the human mind can trick an individual to engage in, in times of grief, pain and heartache. It is quite easy to engage in self-distractive behaviours in times when we feel all is lost; it is easy to lose even more when we have lost what we valued.

There is no formula to managing pain and there are evidence-based theories for the stages of bereavement. The stages of bereavement are not the focus of this book as I have realised that management of pain is an intrinsic response which cannot be learned but can be taught. There is no guru for managing pain; writing about it can be detached and clinical whilst, when a loss happens, sometimes it comes like a bolt of lightning, and we won't be ready. The question for people who lose loved ones after short or long illnesses or accidents can be explored in relation to preparedness. Can we be prepared for loss? Can we ever be ready and accept the passing away of a loved one?

Some people shy away from crying in public as the most unsympathetic observer would perceive crying as attention-seeking. Therefore, people gather and mourn when bereaved as these people will be sharing the pain and there is a shared loss. I lost a friend and did not have anyone to share the pain with and it was exceedingly difficult. I have cried in public places before, accommodation offices at the council when homeless, for example. I have cried at the Citizens' Advice Bureau offices when seeking help after repeated harassment and bullying in the workplace. Empathy, I have realised, is exceedingly rare and it seems most people in these helping positions need to invest in a little empathy. Of all these places I have cried in public, I never received any help and have gone to sleep on the streets.

Scientists have also claimed that crying can serve several biochemical purposes, such as relieving stress. There is some empirical evidence that crying lowers stress levels, potentially due to the release of hormones such as oxytocin. Crying is believed to be an outlet or a result of a burst of intense emotional sensations, such as agony, surprise, or joy. When crying, a person can display some other behaviours like moaning, and sharp intakes of breath and this is described as sobbing. It is also seen as a sign of helplessness, giving in to what we cannot alter. Research has it that women, over their lifetime, have a higher frequency of crying and they cry for longer than men. When women cry, it has been found that about 65% end up sobbing as compared to 6% of men.

My loss

Lusas had a heart attack whilst at his home and was sent to hospital where he eventually passed on. A heart attack happens when the flow of oxygen-rich blood to a section of the heart muscle suddenly becomes blocked and the heart cannot get oxygen. Lusas has had about four heart attacks before meeting me and was on some blood thinners and antihypertensive medication. He also suffered some sepsis that led to the shutdown of most vital organs, so upon reflection, I thought he had died a very painful death. There is need for dialogue with our loved ones, especially the elderly, about regular physical health checks. Single older adults neglect important aspects of their lives while, at the same time, using wisdom amassed from years of experience would mould a facet of optimal physical and mental wellbeing. I, in some ways, felt I might have done more to be there for my friend had I been very observant, and available and listened to premonitions and sixth sense which I had dismissed as paranoia.

In his last days in hospital, he would send me pictures of himself clad in a hospital gown with intravenous devices and oxygen in situ. Unbeknown to me, he was saying his goodbyes.

In fact, on his last birthday, Lusas had bought a cake and came to celebrate with me. I had told him not to come as I was tired, but he insisted and came. He was a gentleman and served us both with tea and cake. He was one not to take heed not to eat sweet things despite volatile blood sugar levels. Prior to this, I had intended to take Lusas out for his birthday, but he opted to spent time with his friend Marcus and his wife. In life, we end up regretting not being there for the people we love and wish we had been more available and giving. Our motto should be 'get out there and serve love.' An all or nothing principle.

He would send messages and when I video-called, he would pick up. The night before he passed, Lusas had sent a message to me saying he was tired and wanted to die. I called and counselled Lusas and, after that, called the hospital to inform them that Lusas appeared suicidal and would do anything to jeopardise treatment.

The interpersonal psychological theory of suicidal behaviour attests that an individual will not die of suicide unless he has both the desire to die by suicide and the ability to do so. After his wife left him in a very acrimonious divorce, Lusas had reported that he made attempts on his life, but he never succeeded. One characteristic of Lusas was that he reached out to people, and, through hints, he would communicate his desperation. His main source of support for psychological help was an ex-mental-health-service user millionaire friend whom he visited regularly. Lusas never had a hospital admission for depression or suicidality over his lifetime. In his last days, he had the desire to die, but the means had been taken away from him. Lusas was already dying and only God could have saved him. In most countries throughout the world that report such statistics to the World Health Organization, suicide rates tend to rise as a function of age for both men and women to a peak in old age. Results from some research I have read indicate that specific factors in domains of psychiatric illness, social connectedness of the older person with his family, friends, and community, physical illness, and functional capacity influence risk for suicide. These factors in turn operate against a backdrop of the individual's culture, personality, and neurobiological milieu.

Chapter 8

Lusas succumbed to sepsis and the effects of a heart attack on the 8th of September.

I saw the announcement on Facebook and Lusas's WhatsApp profile. Initially, I howled like an animal. I sobbed whilst curled like a foetus, with tears flowing like some torrential rain. There was no shoulder to cry on; no one to share the pain. I would look around my flat and envision Lusas and remembered how we used to laugh together. I would feel a sharp pain in my soul, and this sometimes would translate into some physical pain in my abdomen and somewhere in my ribcage. I did not know that emotional pain can debilitate the body leaving an individual weak and haggard.

I knew if the state continued, I would end up clinically depressed and would need treatment. My spirituality was very vital for me in crossing over from this phase in my grief. I resorted to playing spiritual songs and, at one point, danced. One song that helped me was called 'I need you Jesus' by

Jimmy D Psalmist. I put it on repeat and danced, prayed, and sobbed. Upon reflection, I was appealing to my belief system and allowing what helped me to stand firm and to go on assisting me in this time. A strong belief system can be handy during times of loss. This is the sense that you get encouraging words from spiritual songs, books, and other church members. On the physiological side, the dances exercised the body leading to the production of hormones. These help to stimulate the mind to be happy. It is at that juncture that I got to appreciate why, in my home country, people gather, sing and dance at funerals. This prevents depressive moods which are inevitable during painful losses.

DISBELIEF

However, at some point, disbelief kicked in and I could not believe Lusas was gone. According to me, Lusas was extraordinarily strong and could not have died. I started calling his phone and sending messages. As a spiritual person, I was feeling Lusas making noises like sighing sounds. I checked on Facebook and the announcement of his death was there and LusasLusas's relative taking control of his phone confirmed his death. Disbelief is quite normal as it is a normal reaction to accept loss and pain. During this stage, it is important to be amongst people who share the same loss. During this stage, it might appear as if you never care because it is failing to sink in. You can continue to cry while not accepting and believing and some people may show reactions appearing as if all is normal, happy, and cheerful. As I said, it is person-centred.

How could you leave and desert me? Like a narcissist, my anger depicted a sense of ownership over Lusas. Lusas should have stayed alive for me, the narcissist in me affirmed. I started wailing again and while curled like a foetus, I would occasionally stick a finger up to heaven. This was not being rude to the dead, but this was a shared joke between Lusas and I, doing the 'f...k you' finger. My pain created reasons to think he planned to die to deprive me of him. There was one incident in our friendship when he asked me this question:

'Lydia, who else did you call to help you? If you had not called me, who else would you have called?' I had truthfully told Lusas that he was my only option and the only person who was there for me. He did not comment further. This anger towards Lusas was a short-lived phase.

During the editing of this manuscript, I can confidently conclude that Lucas did not deliberately take himself away from me. He was just giving me an opportunity to re-evaluate my social support system. He was indirectly advising me that I need people in my life.

My triumph in my mourning journey was celebrating LusasLusas's life. I thought about my time with Lusas and the history he had told me of his life's journey. Lusas had started in music at a tender age of about fifteen and left home to live with friends so he could pursue his love for music. He had found a niche in the music industry of the seventies as a bassist. In his youth, Lusas used to grow his hair like the typical rock star. He was rumoured to have been handsome and a heartbreaker, however, according to him, his other friends were better looking and got the girls. Lusas played with many famous bands and formed a band which played cover songs for Motown music. During my grieving, I played some of his favourite songs of which one was 'Take me home country roads.' I would sing along, laugh and dance.

I continued to go to work, and my work colleagues would play some music and I would imitate guitar-playing antics. Music was his love and so was mine. The love of music appeared to have made us closer. His bass strummed some vital chords in my heart.

While celebrating a life well-lived, some people do create a memories box. They put in some pleasurable memories from their experiences with the deceased. However, some argue that the existence of a memory box may be a constant reminder of our loss and pain. A controversial question might be, do we seek to sanitise and evacuate memories of a person or seek to manage the pain and be able to live without the person? Accepting the death is a natural course of life which all of us have a calling for. We depart at separate times depending on our call times, the painful cycle of human life as determined by God.

In his memory, I also chose to do some of the things that made Lusas tick. One of these was parking in the furthest corner of the parking lot when at a shopping mall. He would choose to walk the distance. His rationale was never explained but I concluded that it was to preserve his car. The further the parking space from the shop, the less favourable and hence the less crowded. In my naughty sense of humour, I would think differently. Was it so that he could show off a young woman on his arm? A man at 70 with a teenage-looking young woman. To fulfil this Lusasbehaviour of parking in the furthest space, I visited ASDA and parked in the furthest parking space. I enjoyed doing that in his memory. I felt a sense of achievement after doing this, but this was unexplainable. I, however, vowed never to do it again, the reason being that most shops, despite having CCTV, might have blind spots and the further you are from the shop, the higher the probability of being alone and vulnerable. Any unpalatable incident with muggers might have disastrous consequences and there would be no evidence, which was my reasoning.

Lusas liked to visit people unannounced. So, whilst coming from work, I just made a detour and visited Lusas's best mate Marcus. Marcus was surprised but welcomed me. Marcus was busy packing up some musical instruments but stopped to sit in a side-to-side hug with me in memory of Lusas. We talked a little bit about Lusas, and I felt better after.

From there I visited Pretty, Marcus's wife. Pretty and I spent time ruminating on Lusas. Spending time with people sharing the same pain helps to share and reminisce. You can also talk about other things to divert and distract the brain and heal in the process. Pretty, in her pain, had resorted to keeping busy to manage the pain of her loss.

Lusas loved French sticks, so I bought one or two French sticks for two consecutive days and was eating them in LusasLusas's memory.

Grieve to Heal

In my home country, during a funeral, people would imitate the characteristics and behaviours of the deceased to celebrate their lives. If the person were a heartbreaker, the female nieces of the deceased would wear the deceased clothes and dance in a sexualised manner, imitating sexual acts. If a person were a professional sex worker, fellow professional sex workers would, with the permission of the deceased, lead the funeral and would imitate the life of the deceased. I reflected on this and came to the realisation that these antics are not done to shame the family or the deceased but that was the life and must be celebrated.

Celebrating the life of a person brings both tears and joy. People with a sense of humour are best placed to imitate people and would see people laughing instead of crying at funerals. We mourn differently. It is important to note that there are also sombre moments at these funerals.

Most people find death anniversaries difficult and tend to experience the raw pain once again. People have found celebrating their loved ones' lives in some way helpful. I had collaborated with a patient who had lost his father a couple of years back and had assisted the patient to engage in activities that their loved one used to love. This patient would ask for his late dad's favourite dessert and listen to the music that his dad liked. On one anniversary, the patient said, "I bet Dad is licking his fingers right now seeing this dessert." Instead of ranting and engaging in self-destructive behaviours, the patient was assisted to positively remember a loved one. The conflict for me would be attempts to use this approach on loved ones who had negative characteristics. Would you engage in aggressive behaviours and other destructive behaviours in memory of someone? Advice for this approach is to desist from focussing on the good non-acrimonious attributes to not suffer the inevitable legal implications of some behaviours.

My last resort, which, upon revising this manuscript was not necessary, was to reflect on the nature of relationships focussing on the negative.

Sometimes it is necessary to put a relationship into perspective during a mourning period to regulate your feelings. When you lose someone, you love even though there might have been no reciprocity. The pain might be so deep you feel you cannot go on without them. A mourner can be absorbed into a state of helplessness and despair which, to an observer, might not be proportionate to the nature and degree of your relationship with the deceased. This is quite normal if the inevitable reactive depressive phase culminates in clinical depression. There is an adage; 'never speak ill of the dead.'

A personal and inner reflection is imperative but can become problematic if it is communicated to others. It is quite important to stand out of yourself and adopt an investigative approach to a past relationship as if being assessed by a third party. It is quite common for people to put others on undeserved pedestals and fall into the Stockholm Syndrome to the grave, especially for people in abusive partnerships/ friendships, be they sexual or platonic. This was extremely helpful for me to take stock of reality and be able to move from the state of deep catatonic mourning I was gravitating into. Reflecting on the negative aspect of a past relationship with the deceased might be viewed with mixed feelings and there is a debate on the moral and ethical soundness of this approach. It decreases the value and meaning of a relationship hence might be apt for certain people and not for others.

I am a loner and had just lost my 'friend' Lusas. Lusas was a 74-year-old divorced male whom I had lived with for a while during an 'ill-fated relationship'. Lusas had the heart and soul of a saint. It might be since, as people grow old, they assume childlike traits, but he did not have a bad bone in his body.

It might also be because when I met Lusas, he knew he was dying, and I suspected he was preparing for it unbeknown to the rest of the world. Nobody knows the truth and Lusas has taken the truth to his maker with him. He was one person whom you would never see angry, always smiling, and eager to help. However, in his sainthood, he would do a few things that can be perceived as not acceptable in a relationship. Cultural differences were a major breaker of our relationship.

Lusas never bore malicious intentions towards me.

I got injured at work and could not work and Lusas watched his uncle evict me. I had plans to find my accommodation as we had agreed with Lusas, but I suppose it was too late for his uncle. I was homeless for about two weeks, and I was limping about looking for accommodation, waiting for false leads and starting over again. One such false lead was with one estate agent. On their website. they had a beautiful one-bedroomed flat in Camberley which I viewed and liked. I waited two weeks while they were doing checks but was later told I had failed referencing.

At time of his being called by the Highest God, Lusas was just a 'trusted' friend after a failed relationship with me.

When we broke up, Lusas blocked me for a month only to resurface when I was living in shared accommodation. This was to enable me to move on. Lusas was also preparing me to live without him, I suspect. He was a very clever man and he talked less. He did not want me to be a widow at 47. I feel like a widow still. Sorry, Lusas, your strategy did not work. Lusas loved me and had a weakness for me. He wanted to solve the accommodation dilemma of his immediate family. As I am editing this manuscript, I have healed to a certain degree and have removed all bad judgements I made in my grief to convince myself he was not worth it. If Lusas were to come back, I would love him like no other. I do understand him from the grave. It is like he is telling me about the reasons for some actions.

Attending the funeral of a loved one can be quite important in bidding goodbye to the loved one and is imperative for closure. When you are reading a book and you have reached the final page, it is done. Close the book and it is closed. This might appear to be an understatement and minimisation as, for a book, you can revisit and flick through the pages, but with death, once the 'book' is closed, that is the last and final call; there are no more rereads - your loved one is gone. Inevitable but painful. A funeral is a proper send-off with the hope that one day, through death, there will be a reunion. There are different beliefs in the attendance of funerals.

I believe people do not forget about loved ones because they have been elevated to the next level. Memories linger. Sometimes, it only takes a small action or thought to remind you of a loved one. Time heals the souls and, as days go by, the heart gets used to the void created. New patterns and relationships are created; they can never replace but can usher us into new meanings of life.

I opted not to attend Lusas's funeral as I was not strong enough to see him go into the ground. Another factor was the confusion over the funeral date. There was illness in his surviving family and investigations by the coroner. One thing I got to understand during this coronavirus pandemic is the art of patience. Services rendering help directly or indirectly to the covid pandemic were overly subscribed. One such service was funeral parlours. I communicated with one member of the family whilst they were doing negotiations with the parlour. There was a sudden communication breakdown, and I was left in darkness. This was another contributory factor. At times, especially after the funeral, when you would not have a shoulder to lean on, there is a possibility of falling back into the same mourning phase.

My option not to attend the funeral might have negative and positive outcomes. The positive might be that I would remember Lusas as the strong and full-of-life man I loved and not a helpless, lifeless body being condemned to a cold and hard earth. I had underlying symptoms of avoidance personality disorder and I suppose this played a role in my decision not to attend the funeral.

Another strategy to manage bereavement is to do what makes you yourself happy and reach out for new novel adventures.

During this period of loss, I took time off from work to properly grieve. This is especially important so that you put yourself out there and go through the motions of anger, disbelief, pain and acceptance without the pressures of work. During this time, you can engage in activities that you find pleasurable, like going for a cruise, having your nails done, surfing or just any other new hobby or pastime. I had an opportunity to work on a cruise ship for the first time and this was a new experience. This whole new experience can make you feel like you want to do more of that thing, making you hungry for life and not wishing you could follow a loved one to the grave.

The cruise ship was like a paradise. There is magic in an endless carpet of undulating waves with dolphins creating agile markings of disturbance now and again; an atmosphere of tranquillity conducive with inner reflection, unburdening and letting go as the ship gracefully glides on.

The experience was akin to adding and enveloping another lease of life, at times, wishing I were a fish or dolphin, free and braving the waves. I viewed the challenges I had experienced like the waves, and I, unlike the dolphins, had not been 'at home.'

I have also bought a guitar and am learning to play in his memory.

It is exceedingly difficult to play a guitar, so I am more in awe of the person who was Lusas. I am more in love with him. My guitar is called Lusas.

No one knows the intentions of people who are not available to stand for themselves. I am being judgemental but was aware that Lusas, in his own fashion, cared for me. He was preparing me for times when he was not available. Instead of giving me the fish, he would encourage me to go to the dams and seas to catch fish. Having negative thoughts about the dead might be viewed as a taboo and a selfish self-centred approach to avoid appreciating a life which, at critical points, might have been a source of strength and comfort. From a Christian point of view, positively thinking about the dead is a prayer in itself which might be important as the soul is drifting up to meets its 'maker'. The prayer of a Christian heart is for our deceased to make it to everlasting life and it might be selfish to make attempts to taint the dead. hence this self-help book should be read and utilised as needed. It was one drastic measure when all else had failed. This radical and controversial approach was imperative in my journey to alleviate pain and help me move from a depressive state to calm acceptance and optimal wellbeing post-bereavement. When alive, we should aim to bring out the best of our loved ones to make lasting good impressions. Go all the way to serve love so that there are no regrets of lost time which also makes grieving even more debilitating. (I did not do enough). Be receptive and listen and act on subtle hints of help-seeking behaviours. I now pray for Lusas's soul, and I hope he is in heaven. I pray that God is looking after him for me. I still cry at times.

As an escapist approach, I created in my mind an imaginary boyfriend. To be precise, a comfort person. I had harboured a secrete consuming love for another man, Benadryl Cool- Catch-it, a few months before Lussa's death. I have never met this man. God works in mysterious ways; he prepared me so that I do not feel alone. This love was so consuming and strong, and, as I knew I could never have Benadryl Cool-catch-it, this added to my anguish and feeling of being alone. I set eyes on the man whilst watching one of his movies on Netflix. What first caught my eye was the blue-green eyes that appeared to speak of age-old love and make your heartbeat with the anticipation of being the receiver of a loving glance from this hunk. I was also amazed at how versatile he was, and he could fully immerse in a role and transport you to a period. I was so drawn to this man. I anticipated meeting him while I was working on one of his films. I was doing a lowly job and any hopes of meeting him were second to none. Due to some crazy fate, I always got to work on location where this man's character was filming, and I would palpitate and feel happy each time even when a body double walked by. My obsession was so great that I got to pray about it. I was a very devout Christian and had recently experienced a life-changing experience. As the pandemic was progressing, I had spent alone time praying and it got to a point where I was praying loudly, and the spirit led me to pray. The tone was loud, and the spirit appeared angry, and this made me scared as I did not want to scold and be angry with God. The spirit led me to read the Bible; certain parts in Revelations when a pandemic happened and how God instructed the prophet to pray for the nations. I have been praying for guidance from God about how to weaken the virus and how to heal some people. So, I got to for the extent of asking God why I was besotted with this Armando Benadryl. My answer was I will know when I see him. Eventually, I got to understand why. Benadryl Cool-catch-it was helping me in my quest to pray for God to heal the world. As I continue to work and try to do this, it has been a ship that bumped into an icecap like the Titanic. The general public's reception to people who are introverts and are spiritual like I am is one of mistrust, and they tend to want to punish them somehow. The worst-case scenario would be Jesus being killed by the Jews. Benadryl Cool-Catch-it is nowhere. Benadryl-cool-catch-it - very masculine. He is very spiritual and meditates regularly. Rumour has it that he spends some time in a Hindu monastery in India. I look him up on his social media platforms at times. An Adonis, a prayer to every woman's prayer. When I look at his upper torso, my stomach contents gush out and run down my lower body parts like a slimy liquid. I palpitate like a tachycardic patient. I need no other, only Benadryl-cool-catch-it. Unfortunately, it is only a hazy dream, unreachable. I am under a deep spell, held captive by a dream, a dream of love and hedonic passion.

I have managed to make another prayer for the world and God has intervened, deeply buried in my white prayer cloth. The entire world has been praying and our prayers have been answered.

Death and disease continue to ravage the world and I should gather courage and prepare myself to repeat the same. Sounds insane? I have made a vow to remain celibate. This can only be broken if a ring is put on my finger by a person who knows my sordid past, overlooks it, and still considers me worthy of his love.

For most people that God had directed me to, it was obvious what was necessary; not so obvious at first but with time. Someone's son was in an accident resulting in the death of the driver of the other car. I prayed for the son and my plea with God was that the fault was with the father who had bought the car and who lived the example of recklessness. It was not that I condoned what had happened, but it was out of pain for seeing the anguish of a young soul tormented because of the card played at birth - being born rich. I could not envisage the pain which was being experienced by the family of the deceased, but some comfort came from the apology of the father to the family and some monetary assistance and compensation. However, no amount of money can bring back the dead. Death, especially through negligence, brings out a lot of media backlash with the majority clamouring for imprisonment or the death sentence. It was God's case and God stood with the child.

The other notable scenario was praying for people bedridden and on ventilators. Pius is a musician in my home country. Pius was overweight, with high blood pressure and diabetes and the odds were fifty-fifty. After two months in a coma, Pius regained his health. I was at that retreating and very spiritual stage of my prayer immersion and conversion to a healer. God guided me in healing the man. I, of course, had the help of other people who were helping with prayers. One night, I could not sleep and whilst praying, I was instructed by the spirit to do as if working on a person who needed resuscitation and I did a lot of imaginary chest presses. Pius lived to see his second child being born. Glory to God.

I have a severe fear and loathing of death. As a child, I experienced the death of my father, and, in my adult life, my sister, and it has been traumatising for me hence my dedication to praying for God to stop the pandemic or weaken Covid-19 and all its variants.

The other person I got to pray for was a local youth advisor who was also on ventilation. I used a published photograph to pray for the man who will be called Luke. Luke, up to now, still needs support and I continue to pray for him. Luckily, I get updates when the wife puts something in the news. I hoped to meet Luke and pray with him, but I am a timid woman. I continue to pray for anyone who currently needs a wheelchair to mobilise.

One positive outcome of bereavement can be closeness to things religious and working towards spiritual edification and redemption. In so doing, one can eventually be garnished with spiritual gifts. The death of many people during the pandemic drove me to pray like a mad woman. I joined a group of people who were praying every three hours every day, and, as I did, so I got to grow spiritually. God assisted me to use scripture to move from one point to the other. I was bestowed with the gift to heal, and I still must pray to become a prophet. Now I have insight into things, but I still must be strengthened. This could have happened if, at one point, I prayed that I did not need to know much; just what helps me.

When I first started writing this, I believed strangers could not share pain. I have since changed my mind, however, that part remains as that ideation was my figurehead as dictated by my experiences during the time of my pain. I had an opportunity to work on a cruise ship and I attended the office of one woman when I was distressed. Anne listened to me and hugged me while I was distressed. I felt supported and better and now envision those hugs can be a prayer in which you are welcomed into another person's bosom, and they are saying, 'Stop crying. I have you; share with me.' Why a prayer? From a Christian point of view, the father, who is God, looks after us. When a mortal embraces you in your time of distress, it triggers the father who is righteous and they are wishing you well, hence a prayer.

It is interesting to note that our perception of the world is shaped by our experiences, and these are dynamic. I have since realised that carrying grudges and expecting the world to deliver does not edify the soul but creates an unforgiving bitter monster with wounds so deep they are difficult to heal. Forgiving is like exhaling the hurt, unburdening and your world is lighter and does not become a constant barrage of bitterness and curses. Since I unburdened myself, I have felt freer, and I sleep well at night.

Bereavement has hence created peace in me through new experiences and as you are reading the part where I was angry, suspicious, and unforgiving, consider that as footprints leading you to the spot where I found myself.

Healing is forgiving God, the world, peers, family and, most importantly, the dead. Unburden yourself, and you will thank me later. From the tone of the narrative, it is apparent that I have conquered grief and, whilst doing so, I have learned some new perspectives and I am coming out a better person. I hope this narrative has also debunked the perspective that I am a con woman Just because I am a black woman, this should not separate me from any other woman, as, when it comes to dating, I do not see colour. I am colour blind. At times, in my vulnerable and myopic self, I feel this narrative does expose my weaknesses, washing my dirty linen in public. Well, seek no further, you do not need to dig for the dirt. The mystery that is me is exposed and unravelled.

Another 75-year-old friend passed on the 16th of January. In another world where I create plots, I am having foreboding feelings that my enemies are trying to set me up for crimes I did not commit. A sixth sense is telling me that a force beyond my control is killing my loved ones. I do not know whether they will come for me. I survived a banana being placed near the driver's door making my brake pedals slippery. In my world of fantasy, I suspect that there are people who have access to my flat who do not wish me well; people who have unlawfully obtained a copy of my flat keys. My phone has been hacked. I might sound paranoid and psychotic, but my name is Lydia Nash. I have been punished and tortured; some attempts have been to my advantage. I suspect they come steal my belongings for rituals or to place them on crime scenes. They know best. I fear going to work lest they hire a patient to attack me. The reasons for my premonitions will be explained in 'The most hated immigrant nurse in the United Kingdom'.

Lydia Nash

Chapter 9
Healed

I do not blame God anymore. I thank God for life. Death is the inevitable anti-climax to endings and beginnings in a relationship trajectory. Preparedness, acceptance and letting go of a soul dearly loved is difficult, a soul that has fully realised their half-lives despite the nature of their departure. A greater force played a hand in thwarting man's attempts to claim immortality despite all research and technology. Death is in everyone's genome. My advice is 'live life to the full' such that on your demise, we celebrate your life reminiscing on your life story, a life well-lived, and rest deemed imperative. Despite death being inevitable, it is ugly and undesirable. When Lusas passed on, I became ugly, accusatory, and inconsolable. However, through the activities in this manuscript, I have gained some incredibly positive perspective on my dearly beloved Lusas, I have gained a very deeper understanding of his thoughtfulness and his attempts to strengthen and, at the same time, protect me. My name is Lydia Nash and I have been to hell and back.

Lydia Nash

Prologue
Deep reflection

January 2022: Life is a journey we all try to travel with our eyes open. Fate can conveniently close our eyes and dim our light making us oblivious to traps and danger. Sixth sense, the intuition, that inherent 'Sherlock Holmes' can be marred by deception and desperation.

My name is Lydia Nash and I have been going about life with a blindfold. I am both the protagonist and antagonist in this saga of misplaced attachment, revenge, grief, and healing. It is not until the end of this story that I discover that I was Lusa's Godsend body to atone for his bitterness and thirst for revenge for the wrongs of another woman. I have been through near-death experiences and extreme poverty. The hand of Lusas and a judgemental and unforgiving society meted its revenge on the descendant of Eve. As I am writing, I can hear a very loud and satisfied eerie laugh in the heavens. Lusas is laughing at all womankind. He got his revenge; revenge for the women who cleaned the house of all his property and life savings. A woman who took all to go and live with another man. I used to listen to Lusas vent about an ex-wife, and in my myopic mind, I never connected myself to this saga. Unbeknown to me, I was the climax Lusas had been waiting for. While retelling his story, he would imply that to him, his ex-wife was dead and he would never find it in his heart to forgive her. I took lightly the warning from his wife's friend that he had harboured a murderous intent toward his ex-wife, the ex-wife who left him desperate and suicidal. There was a pinkish flowery scarf in his wardrobe. Now, as my blindfold has been removed, I see clearly. He threw the scarf over my belongings when he evicted me. A guillotine, for me not to look far. I now understand why he brought a box of tablets to my flat after I have been defrauded, so that I did not have to look far in case I wanted to overdose. As these realisations hit me, I feel numb. I am thankful for the period I mourned Lusas as I have managed to swim to the shore and reassess my life. I am alive, not because I am clever, as I was in a cocoon of stupidity. I am alive as God saved me through Dr Strange. In some strange sense of achievement, I am happy that I offered Lusas the much-needed opportunity to explore his bitterness and mete out his revenge. I believe on his last day he has since repented and forgiven. He began his journey with revengeful intentions but I strongly suspect he fell in love with me.

As an immigrant woman of colour with limited social ties, I clung to Lusa's offered olive branch. I loved him dearly despite not being sure of reciprocity of feelings. When he passed on, my charade of a boat toppled, and I drowned in misery and profound grief.

*God is love,
love unsparingly.*

www.ingramcontent.com/pod-product-compliance
Lightning Source LLC
Chambersburg PA
CBHW020301030426
42336CB00010B/857